LOOK AND FIND

Disney's
THE
HUNCHBACK
OF NOTRE DAME

ILLUSTRATED BY JAIME DIAZ STUDIOS

COVER ILLUSTRATED BY DARRELL BAKER

WRITTEN BY NANCY L. MCGILL
AND TRUDY NICKELS

Published by
Louis Weber, C.E.O.
Publications International, Ltd.
7373 North Cicero Avenue
Lincolnwood, Illinois 60646

© Disney Enterprises, Inc.

Manufactured in U.S.A.

8 7 6 5 4 3 2 1

ISBN 0-7853-1823-2

Look and Find is a registered trademark
of Publications International, Ltd.

PUBLICATIONS INTERNATIONAL, LTD.

High above the city of Paris rises the bell tower of Notre Dame. Every day the majestic bells ring out, as if by magic. Only a few have seen the mysterious bell ringer, Quasimodo, who lives high up in the tower. This is the tale of Quasimodo, his friends, and his master.

In the picture, count the times you see these characters.

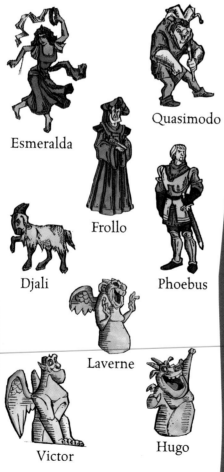

Esmeralda

Quasimodo

Frollo

Djali

Phoebus

Laverne

Victor

Hugo

Answers are in the back of the book.

PHOEBUS

To make his bell tower feel more like home, Quasimodo has filled it with wonderful things he found or made. Can you find these things in Quasimodo's bell tower?

This candelabrum

This clay bowl

This trunk

Wind chime

This goblet

This statue

This wooden carving

This footstool

Quasimodo loves to watch all of the actions in Paris below from the bell tower. Most of all, he wants to go out and join the fun. Today is the biggest celebration of the year, the Festival of Fools. Look around to find these people who are doing the things Quasimodo would like to do if he were out there.

Phoebus

Clopin

Esmeralda

Antoinette

Fifi

Desdemona

Philippe

Pierre

At the Festival of Fools, up is down and black is white and back is front and in is out and everybody appears to be somebody else! There seem to be quite a lot of Jacques roaming the streets at the festival. Can you find them all?

Frère Jacques

Jacques and Jill

Jacques-in-the-box

Jacques of hearts

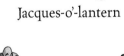

Jacques-o'-lantern

Jacques Sprat

Jacques-of-all-trades

Run, Esmeralda! Dodge and duck. Use your speed and all your luck! Frollo wants Esmeralda captured after she helps Quasimodo at the Festival of Fools. Kind-hearted and quick on her feet, Esmeralda is a show-stopper. As Esmeralda runs through the festival, find these guards who want to catch her.

Pierre

René

Henri

Jean-Claude

Christophe

Dominique

Marc

Luc

Esmeralda follows Quasimodo to his bell tower, where they become fast friends. Quasimodo shows her his wood carvings. She wonders at the beautiful detail of his miniature model of Paris and laughs to see everyone she knows represented by a carefully carved doll. Look to see the dolls Esmeralda likes best.

Andre

Petit

Georgette

François

Felice

Nicolette

Louis

After a long day in the streets of Paris, gypsies of all shapes and sizes go to the Court of Miracles. Every night is like a festival here! Can you find these gypsies who have ended the day with an evening of play?

Poco Paco

Castanet Mariette

Green Grizabella

Zooming Zeke

Chapeau Joe

Omelette Yvette

Asleep Philippe

Soapy Sam

Paris is burning! Quasimodo's sanctuary is not even safe from the evil Frollo. Outside on the parapet, Quasimodo is cornered by Frollo as he tries to rescue Esmeralda. Look out at Paris and find these people— and animals—battling to save Notre Dame.

Phoebus

Achilles

Clopin

Marc

Isabelle

Djali

Georges

BOOKS

Three cheers for Quasimodo! He helped return happy times to all the people of Paris. But there is more to this happy ending than meets the eye. Look around and see if you can find these other happy things.

The blue bird of happiness

A burst of confetti

A happy camper

Merry Mary

A roly-poly puppy

A happy reunion

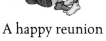

A bouquet of flowers

Bakery

Quasimodo's name means "half-formed." Go back to the woodcut story to find these other half things.

Half crown
Half-dollar
Half a heart
Half-moon
Half cup
Half-time
Half shell

The bells are not the only things that make music in Quasimodo's bell tower. Can you find these other musical things?

Violin
Tambourine
Flute
Drum
Harp
Accordion
Horn

From his view, Quasimodo sees some children making mischief. Can you find their playful pranks, too?

Swinging on a festival banner
Making faces behind
a soldier's back
Stowing away on a fishing boat
Dancing on a rooftop
Hitching a ride on a vendor's cart
Playing king and queen

Everything is wrong-way-up on Topsy Turvy Day! Return to the festival to find these upside-down items.

A fire-breather
An upside-down cake
A banner
A fool's mask
A goblet
A bat

At the Festival of Fools, Esmeralda proves how quick she can be. Go back to the festival and find these other quick things.

Quicksand
A quick draw
Rabbit
Someone with a hotfoot
Lightning
A quick freeze